DEMCO

Mines and Minié Balls

Mines and Minié Balls

Weapons of the Civil War

by Jean F. Blashfield

A First Book

Franklin Watts
A Division of Grolier Publishing
New York - London - Hong Kong - Sydney
Danbury, Connecticut

Photos ©: Blair Seitz: 29; Corbis-Bettmann: 9, 13, 23, 27 top, 32, 34, 46, 51, 53; Library of Congress: cover, 16, 42; The Museum of the Confederacy: 24; North Wind Picture Archives: 6, 10, 52; Stock Montage: 49; U.S. Army Photograph/Collection of Mathew Brady Photographs: 35, 37; West Point Military Academy: 12, 18, 19, 20, 27 bottom, 28, 54, 55; Courtesy of William Katz: 41.

Library of Congress Cataloging-in-Publication Data

Blashfield, Jean F.
Mines and minié balls: weapons of the Civil War/ by Jean F. Blashfield

p.   cm.—(A First book)
Includes bibliographical references and index.
Summary: Describes the various weapons developed and used during the Civil War, such as longarms, handguns, swords, cannons, naval weapons, and mines, and explores that era as the beginning of modern weaponry.
ISBN 0–531–20273–9
1.   United States. Army—History—Civil War, 1861–1865—Juvenile literature.
2.United States. Army—Weapons systems—History—19th century—Juvenile literature. 3. Confederate States of America. Army—History—Juvenile literature.
4.   Confederate States of America. Army—Weapons systems—History—19th century—Juvenile literature. 5.   United States—History—Civil War,1861–1865—Juvenile literature.[1. Weapons—History—19th century. 2.United States. Army—Weapons systems—History—19th century. 3. Confederate States of America. Army—Weapons systems—History—19th century.] I. Title.II. Series.
E491.B58   1997
623.4'0973'09034—dc20   96–32157
                                                                          CIP
                                                                          AC

CONTENTS

Chapter One
Unprepared

*The bombardment of Fort Sumter in Charleston harbor
marked the beginning of the Civil War.*

The first shot fired in the American Civil War came
from a mortar—a type of very heavy, short-barreled
cannon. It was fired above the walls of Fort Sumter in
the harbor at Charleston, South Carolina, by Confederate

Lieutenant Henry S. Farley at 4:30 A.M. on April 12, 1861. This shot marked the beginning of the war fought to keep the states that formed the United States of America one nation.

When the actual fighting began, both the Union and the Confederacy (the eleven southern states that had seceded from the United States) were certain that the war would last only a few months . . . and each thought it would emerge the winner. The two sides, though, were totally unequal in strength.

The Union army had available the entire U.S. war system of the time. Few of the factories producing arms for the United States were in the South. The South had long concentrated on agriculture, while the North had emphasized manufacturing.

The Confederacy had virtually no weapons on hand, no gunpowder stored, and no functioning mines for acquiring iron or factories for making steel. The South seized the federal arsenal at Harpers Ferry, Virginia, and shipped its rifle-making equipment to North Carolina. That was not enough, however. The Confederacy had to quickly set up weapons factories in southern states and also import weapons from other countries.

A TIME FOR CREATIVITY

As the Civil War dragged on, both sides developed new weapons. Many of these innovations still play a role in warfare. They made repeating rifles, telescopic sights, and a machine gun that actually worked. They mounted big guns (artillery) on railway cars and designed revolving gun turrets. And they created "fixed ammunition"— gunpowder and bullet were combined in one case for easy loading.

Other weapons included submarines, land mines, ironclad ships, flame throwers, and floating mines, or torpedoes. They even conducted aerial reconnaissance for the first time, using hot-air balloons. Because some balloons were launched from flat-topped ships, those ships have been called the first aircraft carriers.

GUNPOWDER—THE POWER OF THE WAR

The gunpowder used during the Civil War was a mixture of niter (potassium nitrate), charcoal, and sulfur. Together, these chemicals contain both the fuel and oxygen needed for an explosion.

When the war started, the South could find sulfur, and it could make charcoal from wood, but it had no niter.

The balloon Washington *was launched from the deck of a specially converted ship in the Potomac River to inspect blockade defenses on the coast.*

One man, General George Rains, was responsible for supplying the South with this important chemical, but it was not an easy task. He called on the people of the

Before the war, the making of gun cartridges was strictly men's work, but the need for huge amounts of ammunition meant that even women had to work in factories.

South to dig up the soil beneath outhouses and latrines, because the ammonia in urine that accumulated there could be used to produce niter!

MUSKETS AND MORE

There are two major categories of Civil War weapons: the big guns—artillery, or cannon—and the soldier's own weapons, called small arms. Big and small weapons worked by firing projectiles (bullets) out of a long tube from the force of the explosion of gunpowder. The tube, or barrel, of most weapons was smooth inside, so it was called a *smoothbore*. (*Bore* refers to both the hole running the length of the tube and the internal diameter of that hole.)

Soldiers and hunters had known for a long time that if the inside of their gun's barrel had spiral grooves carved into it, the projectile would spin as it left the muzzle, making it go farther and straighter. Grooves were called rifling, and grooved weapons, both big and small, were called rifles.

For centuries, both soldiers and hunters used a long hand-held weapon called the musket. The advantage of this kind of weapon was that the gunpowder and the iron ball used as a "bullet" could be quickly loaded just by dropping them down the barrel. The ball did not have to be any particular size or shape, as long as it fit inside the barrel. The disadvantages of the musket were that it was not very accurate, and the ball was not very fast because the powder blast went around it, losing much of its explosive energy. The ball's lack of speed kept it from going very far. Also, the musket had to be removed from the shoulder and turned up in order to drop in the ball and powder.

For a rifle, the projectile, which was a cylinder with a point on its end (in other words, what we think of as a

A common rifle-musket used in 1861 was of German manufacture.

bullet) had to be exactly the right width and shape to fit into the grooves. It had to be forced down the barrel with a long probe instead of just dropped in. This bullet took longer to load, which, of course, slowed down the action in battle.

Throughout the Civil War, the most common shoulder weapons were rifle-muskets, a combination of the two kinds of weapons. They loaded through the muzzle but had rifling in the barrel.

MEN—THE MOST IMPORTANT WEAPONS

Large numbers of men were the most important weapon in battle. At first, all soldiers in both the Union and the Confederate armies were volunteers or members of state militias. But within one year, the Confederacy had to

The most important weapons in any army are the people who do the fighting. These are men of the 116th Pennsylvania Infantry after the Battle of Fredericksburg, Virginia, in December 1862.

start drafting men into the army, and within another year, the Union had to do the same.

The men were organized in a traditional manner. The smallest group was the company. This usually consisted of 101 men plus officers. Each company had two musicians—bugle calls and fifes signaled instructions over the din of battle. Ten companies plus officers formed a regiment of volunteers.

Unfortunately, just as weapons could be damaged, so could men. Even a mild wound could do massive damage to the human body. It has been estimated that a soldier's chances of surviving a wound in the Civil War were seven to one. Those who survived often went home minus an arm or a leg.

Chapter Two

Longarms, the Soldiers' Friends

For a man going to war, his closest "friend" was his shoulder weapon, or longarm—a musket, rifle-musket, rifle, or carbine. From the day he joined up, he carried it in parade drill, he practiced marksmanship and speed loading, he polished it, he loved it, and he hated it.

Men who had hunted before the war knew the weapons well. Some even proudly brought their own weapons with them when they signed up. That meant that a few men, especially in the South, carried muskets left over from the American Revolution, eighty years before. But for most volunteers from cities and towns, handling these weapons was a new experience.

GUNS WITH FEET

The basis of both Union and Confederate armies was infantry, soldiers whose main job was to fire longarms—

A Union volunteer as he was equipped in 1861. He carries a long-barreled musket-rifle with a bayonet attached. This picture is a print of a damaged glass photograph taken by famed Civil War photographer Mathew Brady.

these men could be described as guns with feet. They marched in drill, from camp to camp, and into battle as a unit.

The standard infantry weapon for the Union was the Springfield Model 1861 rifle-musket, with a 40-inch (1-m) barrel firing a .58-caliber lead bullet called a minié bullet. (*Caliber* is the diameter of the bullet; this had a diameter of 58/100ths of an inch, or 14.7 mm.) The gun was just under 5 feet (1.5 m) long, plus an additional 21 inches (53 cm) when the bayonet, or blade, was attached to the muzzle. More than 1.5 million Springfields were used by Union troops.

The main Confederate longarms were .577-caliber Enfield rifle-muskets. Authentic Enfields were made by the Royal Small Arms Factory in Enfield, England, but the British government did not allow their arms to be purchased by either side in the American Civil War. The Confederate "Enfields" were actually made by other private manufacturers. They were so reliable and accurate that Northerners bought them, too.

A true marksman with a rifle-musket could hit his target at 600 yards (550 m), but the volunteer soldier was rarely this accurate. The fired bullet moved at relatively

BARRIER TO BREECHLOADERS

In 1811, John H. Hall received a patent for loading a gun through an opening near the trigger. Bullet and powder were dropped into the opening rather than down the barrel. This was the first American breechloader.

Hall's gun was accurate and easy to load, but many military men didn't like change. Union Chief of Ordnance James W. Ripley thought a breechloader would be fired so often that "it would require a mule to carry the ammunition for each soldier—it would be shot away so fast!"

When the Civil War started, many in the Union army used a muzzleloader designed by Ripley himself. He didn't want his weapon to have to compete with a breechloader. Even when President Lincoln commanded him to order the breechloading Sharps rifle for a sharpshooter unit, Ripley delayed.

Gradually, some breechloaders and controversial repeating rifles were used. Ripley was finally forced into retirement by an angry President Lincoln. Within weeks, breechloaders, such as Sharps's above, were in the hands of combat infantry.

low velocity, so it had to be fired upward at an angle if it was to reach its target.

CAVALRY AND CARBINES

Men on horseback carried a variety of carbines. These were lightweight, short-barreled rifles designed especially to be easier to handle on horseback than the longer rifles or muskets. The Burnside carbine, patented by General Ambrose Burnside, was the first American gun to use a metal cartridge (a container to hold gunpowder and bullet).

Christian Sharps's design for a breechloading carbine was simple—the guard over the trigger turned to one side to reveal a chamber into which the cartridge was loaded. Chief of Ordnance James W. Ripley liked this design, and he ordered 80,000 for mounted soldiers. But what the cavalry riders really wanted was the Spencer repeating carbine.

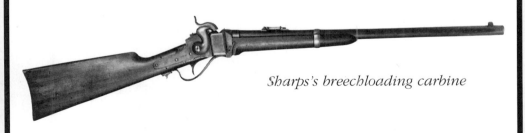

Sharps's breechloading carbine

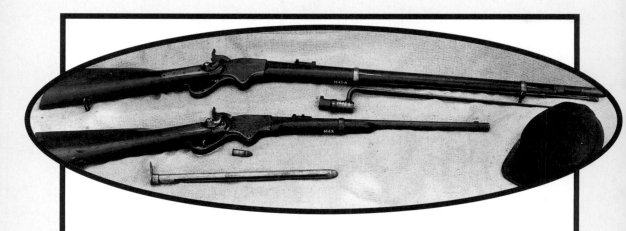

The Spencer repeating carbine, shown with its tube of ammunition beneath the considerably longer Spencer rifle

Christopher Spencer invented his breechloader in 1860. It fired from tubes that held seven cartridges in a row, and the stock held ten or even more tubes. It took more than three years for Spencer to convince the Union generals that the weapon should be used. Once it was ordered in quantity and given to the soldiers, its use was credited with shortening the war. Spencer himself didn't do so well—he produced too many weapons and was forced into bankruptcy after the war. His firm was bought by Winchester Repeating Arms.

Southern cavalrymen preferred the shotgun, usually ones they brought from home. These were shoulder weapons that fired many small pellets at once instead of a single bullet, with the result that a good marksman could injure many people at once.

SHARPS AND SHARPSHOOTERS

In addition to carbines, Christian Sharps had patented the Sharps rifles. These were breechloading, single-shot rifles that could be loaded so fast that the expert could fire up to ten times in one minute. They were the weapons of choice for the Union regiment called Berdan's Sharpshooters. Earlier, the sharpshooters had used Colt repeating rifles, but firing one cartridge could set off the others in the cylinder.

Both Union and Confederate armies had regiments of sharpshooters. Both sides soon found that snipers, as they were also called, were more useful if a few marksmen were attached to a regular regiment for picking off enemy officers. The Confederate sharpshooters preferred the Whitworth rifle, a very accurate, long-range rifle from England, but only a few were imported.

"MINEE BALLS"

With more than fifty different kinds of longarms being used by the two armies, there were many different kinds of ammunition. But the main one—and still the most famous—was the minié bullet, usually called the "minee ball."

The minié bullet was an invention that allowed all soldiers to carry .58-caliber rifles, not just well-trained special soldiers. It was named for one of its developers, Claude-Étienne Minié of the French Army.

Minié's lead, cone-shaped bullet solved the slow-loading problem of rifles. It had a hollow base that expanded into the grooves of the rifle barrel when the gunpowder exploded. The bullet could be smaller than the bore of the rifle, so it took no time to load.

The bullet was prepackaged with just the right amount of gunpowder in a paper cartridge. The gunman tore this open with his teeth and poured the powder into the chamber. He then placed a small percussion cap over a tiny projection with a hole in it. When the hammer struck the percussion cap, a spark went into the powder chamber. The powder exploded, driving the bullet through the barrel.

An infantryman carried between sixty and one hundred cartridges for his rifle-musket as he went into battle. There was not a lot of point in carrying more,

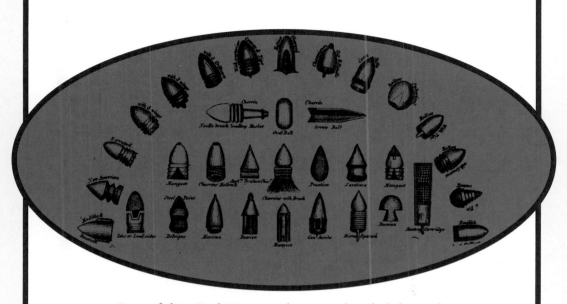

*Part of this Civil War-era drawing detailed the wide
variety of minié balls that had been contemplated
by the French military. Only a few were used in the Civil War.*

because the weapon had to be cleaned after about thirty rounds of firing. The black powder accumulated in the barrel, making it more and more difficult to hammer the ball all the way down to the breech.

During the noise and chaos of battle, stunned infantrymen often threw away their jammed weapons. After the Battle of Gettysburg, more than 35,000 rifle-muskets were found that had belonged to wounded, dead, or frustrated soldiers.

COUNTDOWN TO DEATH

Even with rifled barrels, shoulder weapons of the Civil War were not very accurate. Some soldiers claimed it took their whole weight in ammunition to kill a single enemy. That was an exaggeration, but it was estimated that in various battles a Union soldier used between 100 and 150 bullets for every Confederate soldier hit.

Confederate soldiers ambushing a Union cavalry unit

The Confederate soldiers knew that they had to conserve ammunition. During a skirmish, they often waited patiently until Union soldiers began to run out of bullets. They would then pick them off one by one, making each bullet count.

Union soldiers, on the other hand, were taught to fire as often as they could, which meant that they used up their ammunition fairly quickly. Leander Stillwell of the 61st Illinois Infantry, in battle for the first time at the Battle of Shiloh in April 1862, was patiently waiting for a rebel to come within range of his Austrian-made rifle-musket. His lieutenant ordered him to shoot even if he couldn't see anyone. He later wrote that "the lieutenant was clearly right. Our adversaries were in our front, in easy range, and it was our duty to aim low, fire in their general direction, and let fate do the rest."

Chapter Three
Sidearms—At Close Range

As rifles became easier to use and more accurate, the usefulness of sidearms, such as handguns and swords, began to diminish. But in the Civil War the new had not yet replaced the old.

HANDGUNS

Pistols required a lot of practice to use well, and they were not generally issued, although the Union army ordered fifty-four different kinds during the war. The favorite were the revolving pistols invented by Samuel Colt. Colt's patent had run out a few years before the war, and other manufacturers started making them.

The popular Colt Army Model 1860 revolver was a .44-caliber handgun with a 7.5-inch (19-cm) barrel. Colts could hold six bullets at once, but they had to be cocked between each firing. Such revolvers had a range of about

Combat often came down to one man's sidearm against another's. At right is the Colt .44 Army Pistol, a weapon some soldiers preferred to their longarms.

200 feet (61 m). Like muskets, they frequently jammed as the powder built up inside. Most pistols issued by the Confederate army were copies of Colts and Remingtons.

Also popular was the .36-caliber Model 1861 Navy revolver. This revolver was usually purchased privately because the U.S. government bought only the army model in large numbers. Hand weapons used by the

Navy were usually just like their land counterparts but treated to prevent them from rusting.

Many soldiers, especially Confederates, brought pistols from home when they signed up. These often included dueling pistols, which tended to be more for show than for actual dueling. Most pistols issued by the Confederate army were copies of the northern Colts and Remingtons.

In the long run, infantrymen often ended up getting rid of their pistols. They had to march so often and so far that handguns became just extra weight they had to carry without giving them much benefit.

BAYONETS AND BLADES

Many soldiers carried knives brought from home or bought from blacksmiths. A popular model was the Bowie knife, with a triangular blade up to 18 inches (46 cm) long and a D-shaped handle. These knives tended to be of more use in camp than in combat.

Bayonets—blades attached to the end of rifle-muskets—were still regarded as a major weapon when the war started. In previous wars, musket fire was useful only as a way to start a battle. The actual success

SWORDS FOR SHOW

Swords were basically a thing of the past by the time of the Civil War. Officers and sergeants (noncommissioned officers) wore them primarily as a show of rank.

Cavalrymen carried swords called sabers, which had a slight curve to them. The men learned tactics for their use, especially in pursuing an enemy after their defense was broken. The Battle of Brandy Station in June 1863 was the largest cavalry action of the war. In an engagement that happened virtually by accident, thousands of Union and Confederate horsemen charged each other, with swords in one hand and pistols in the other.

Musicians, who usually carried nothing more lethal than instruments, were often issued a musicians' sword. Shorter than the noncommissioned officers' sword, it was for use if musicians were attacked when performing their secondary duty of carrying wounded men off the field.

Soldiers were usually issued bayonets to fit onto the muzzles of their longarms for use in close combat, but they more often used them as tent pegs instead of weapons.

of battle depended on a close-in charge with deadly blades. As the Civil War began, the soldiers were still trained for such bloody action. But rifle fire changed that.

Governor Joseph E. Brown of Georgia went back to even older times and ways of combat. He decided to furnish the volunteers in his state's militia with pikes. A pike was a 6-foot (1.8-m) wooden staff with an 18-inch (46-cm) blade mounted on the top. The pikes looked impressive to the Georgians who watched the men of their militia march, but they were probably never really used in battle.

Chapter Four
The Cannon's Roar

Big guns, or cannon, could not be carried by an individual. They had to be mounted on a stand or wheels to be moved and fired, and they usually required several people to operate them.

Like shoulder weapons and sidearms, cannon are usually described in terms of diameter of the bore, but they are also defined by the weight of the projectile. A 32-pounder, for example, shoots iron balls or shells that weigh 32 pounds (14.5 kg). Some ammunition was so heavy that crews of men transported it one shell at a time and used pulley systems to load the cannon.

Cannon can be smoothbore, shooting solid iron spherical shot, or rifled, firing elongated projectiles. Civil War cannon were often changed from smoothbore into rifled and even rifled into smoothbore. A rifled smoothbore could take double the weight of ammunition.

Cannons and their spherical shot, or cannonballs, lined up by the Union army at City Point, Virginia, in 1864

Sometimes cannon were given names that caught the public fancy. "Whistling Dick" was a Confederate gun used at the Siege of Vicksburg in 1863. This 18-pounder got its name from the peculiar whistling sound its projectiles made in flight. It had started as a smoothbore but was converted into a rifle.

Although the Confederacy had agents in England buy and ship artillery, most Confederate cannon were captured from the Union. Some were taken as seceding states claimed federal property found within its borders. The remainder were taken during battle. About two-thirds of Confederate artillery were made by the Union.

GOING FOR SIZE AND RIFLING

Rifled cannon were more accurate and had longer range than smoothbore cannon. The most common rifled cannon was the 3-inch (7.6-cm) ordnance gun. Its maneuverability made it the Union commanders' favorite field weapon.

Artillery officers wanted larger and larger weapons. But until shortly before the war, all large weapons had a tendency to crack because of the way the iron, steel, or bronze barrel was made.

In 1857, the U.S. Army bought a manufacturing process developed by Thomas J. Rodman of Indiana. Rodman thought that the old process was at fault because the cannon's metal cooled from the outside in.

A GLOSSARY OF
SMOOTHBORE ARTILLERY

Almost any projectile-firing weapon is a gun, and yet for the cannoneer, a *gun* was a long-barreled, smoothbore weapon that used a heavy charge of powder to fire solid shot at a low angle of elevation. The weight of the projectile varied from 6 to 64 pounds (2.7 to 29.5 kg). The 6-pounders, with a bore of 3.67 inches (9.3 cm), were often rifled to shoot 12-pound projectiles.

The next larger smoothbore cannon was the *howitzer*, which had a shorter barrel. It fired shells with lower charges and at higher elevation. Howitzers had less range than guns. A cannon called the Napoleon was a smoothbore 12-pounder, meant to fire both shot and shell. It replaced both gun and howitzer, so it was often called a *gun-howitzer*.

Mortars had stubby barrels and fired large shells with light charges and high elevations. The force of falling added to the damage. A 13-inch (33-cm) mortar called "Dictator" (shown below) was mounted on the bed of a railway flatcar and hauled

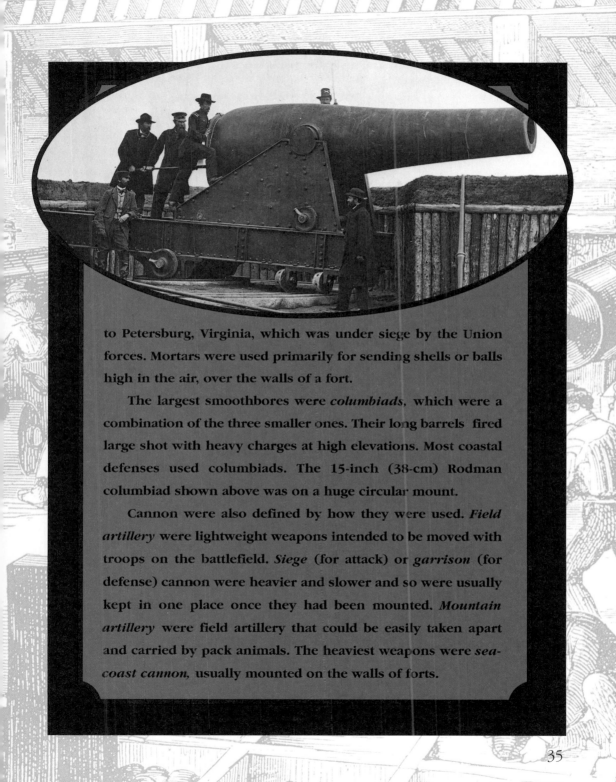

to Petersburg, Virginia, which was under siege by the Union forces. Mortars were used primarily for sending shells or balls high in the air, over the walls of a fort.

The largest smoothbores were *columbiads*, which were a combination of the three smaller ones. Their long barrels fired large shot with heavy charges at high elevations. Most coastal defenses used columbiads. The 15-inch (38-cm) Rodman columbiad shown above was on a huge circular mount.

Cannon were also defined by how they were used. *Field artillery* were lightweight weapons intended to be moved with troops on the battlefield. *Siege* (for attack) or *garrison* (for defense) cannon were heavier and slower and so were usually kept in one place once they had been mounted. *Mountain artillery* were field artillery that could be easily taken apart and carried by pack animals. The heaviest weapons were *seacoast cannon*, usually mounted on the walls of forts.

Rodman developed a way of cooling the metal from the inside out. The process was used especially to make large columbiads.

The largest seacoast guns, permanently mounted on fort walls, had tubes that could weigh more than 50,000 pounds (22,700 kg). Sometimes these guns were placed on swiveling carriages so that they could be turned horizontally as well as raised and lowered for aiming. These huge Rodman guns generally fired only solid cannonballs, which traveled no more than a mile. The shot was so heavy that it had to be handled with a block and tackle—no rapid fire here!

Rodman guns came in a wide variety of sizes, from the 1-pounder to the mammoth 20-inch (50-cm) that at the breech end was almost as wide as the height of a person.

SWAMP ANGEL

The "Swamp Angel" was an 8-inch (20-cm) Parrott gun used to fire into Charleston from a nearby marsh. On the night of August 22, 1863, it shot a 150-pound (68-kg) shell that went an amazing 24,000 feet (7,315 m), scaring inhabitants of the South Carolina city out of their beds. Damage was slight, but it showed that civilians could be killed from long distances.

The defenders had assumed that no big guns could fire from the muddy swamp. In a major engineering feat, Union soldiers had secretly constructed a floating platform that could absorb the recoil of the huge weapon. "Swamp Angel" was fired thirty-five times before it exploded.

Confederate General Beauregard wrote Union General Gillmore, who oversaw the firing, damning him for "the novel measure of turning your guns against the old men, women and children, and the hospitals of a sleeping city, an act of inexcusable barbarity."

Two Blakelys from England were the biggest Confederate cannon—the barrels were 194 inches (5 m) long. They were transported from England mounted vertically in ships so that the ends of their muzzles protruded from the ship as if they were smokestacks. They weighed 27 tons each.

When Charleston was about to be evacuated in February 1865, those Blakelys were blown up by filling them with too much powder. A 2-ton piece of cast iron from one of them blew into the attic of a nearby house, where it remains today.

MORE COMMON RIFLED CANNON

Parrotts were rifled cannon produced by Robert Parker Parrott, an officer who resigned to start his own foundry in 1836. Although most of his weapons were fairly light, he made a 200-pounder (90.7 kg), as well as a 300-pounder (136 kg). Parrott's patent was based on having the tube turned while a reinforcing band around the breech cooled, making it equally strong in all directions.

One officer said the heavy Parrots had "very unequal endurance," meaning they could explode without warning, killing their crews. But they could be made quickly,

A field artillery Parrott gun being fired at distant targets in Virginia

giving the Union weapons as they needed them.

Confederate weapons comparable to the Parrotts were made by John Mercer Brooke, a graduate of the U.S. Naval Academy at Annapolis who resigned his commission to join the Confederate navy. The gun he designed had a sharply tapered barrel, reinforced by several rings of wrought iron.

AMMUNITION

Gunpowder was usually packed in cartridge bags that were various sizes to fit different cannon. Some cannon used what was referred to as fixed ammunition—the powder was attached to the projectile and the two were inserted together.

The oldest type of projectile still used in the Civil War were cannonballs, smooth spheres of solid iron. Cannonballs were used in smoothbore weapons, especially guns and columbiads. Sometimes they had the core removed, leaving them hollow but still sufficiently heavy to damage whatever they hit.

Solid shot was sometimes heated to red hot, then quickly fired at a wooden target, which would be set on fire by this "hot shot." Coastal forts sometimes had special furnaces for use in heating shot to be used against wooden ships, which could easily catch fire.

Shells were hollow cannonballs filled with additional gunpowder, so that when they landed on target they exploded, causing damage both by weight and explosive power.

Even more deadly were grapeshot and canister or case shot—collections of small shot packed into one

One of the most famous incidents of the success of grapeshot was when the guns of Fort Jackson fired on the Union gunboat Iroquois, *killing seven and wounding eight with one shot.*

large shell. When the shell exploded, the smaller balls would disperse over a large area, striking many people at once. Shrapnel was a type of multiple-shot named for its British inventor, General Henry Shrapnel. The name is used today for a fragment of any shell or bomb.

Most cannons were fired with a device called a friction primer. When the cannoneer pulled a rough wire

An artillery unit had many carriages and horses. The gun carriage could be separated from the limber for firing.

across an ignitable material, called friction composition, a spark was created. The spark lighted a small charge of musket powder, which then ignited the main charge deep inside the cannon.

HORSE AND CARRIAGE

Field artillery were mounted on wheeled carriages for traveling and to move in recoil when fired. The carriages were usually pulled by horses to the battlefield. When the guns were lined up in a battery, the horses were taken away—out of the line of fire, if possible Chocks were put against the wheels to keep them from moving, except when the weapon was about to be fired.

The gun carriage was a two-wheeled vehicle, but it could be attached to another two-wheeled vehicle called a limber. The limber had connections for a horse and an ammunition chest that also served as a seat for the driver. A team of six horses pulled the limber and carriage. Special artillery horses had to be able to pull at least 700 pounds (318 kg) over very rough terrain.

Horses in huge numbers were a vital part of an army. Even a light battery of four guns and two howitzers required six caissons (ammunition carriages), a battery (or supply) wagon, and a cart carrying a forge and its bellows for shoeing horses and repairing metal items. This took at least ninety-one horses—all of which had to be fed, groomed, and cared for.

THE CANNONEERS

A gun crew usually consisted of four cannoneers and a gunner. Each had specific movements to carry out, using specific tools, all in a coordinated ballet that would allow the weapon to be fired, moved back out of the line (or "battery"), cleaned, reloaded with gunpowder and projectile, returned to the battery, and fired again—all as quickly as possible. They had to drill regularly to keep in shape for actual combat. It was all done with a shouted sequence of commands: "From Battery . . . Load . . . In Battery . . . Point . . . Ready . . . Fire."

Field guns could be fired about twice a minute, or faster by an experienced crew. Larger cannon usually had to cool off for a few minutes between firings.

The team of cannoneers was well-trained to load, fire, and reload in a smooth rhythm. The weapon was aimed by the gunner.

The North usually had a single kind of gun making up a battery. Because of the problems the Confederates had in obtaining weapons, they rarely had matching weapons in a battery. This made for serious problems of keeping batteries supplied at all times.

Ideally, a single battery consisted of 153 men, including a captain in charge, four lieutenants, two staff sergeants, six sergeants in charge of the ammunition-carrying caissons, twelve gunners (usually ranked as corporals), six artificers able to repair the guns, fifty-two drivers, and seventy cannoneers. In the field, the cannoneers usually had to serve as drivers, too.

CANNON AFLOAT

The Union navy's main job was to keep ships from entering or leaving southern ports. The blockaders were certain the war could be won if they could keep the South from sending cotton abroad to exchange for weapons. In response, the Confederate navy worked to destroy the blockading ships and then sneak out into the ocean from one of the many rivers that indent the southern coastline.

Huge cannon mounted on the decks of ships had

The Monitor, *the Union's first ironclad ship (left), was called a "cheesebox on a raft" because its round gun turret projected above the flat deck. The turret held two Dahlgren cannon.*

been important naval weapons for centuries. The innovation of the ironclad ship made them less useful in the Civil War, but cannon still played a role in the war.

The most famous shipboard guns were the big iron Dahlgrens, designed by Union naval officer John A. B.

Dahlgren. His huge smoothbore cannon were thicker at the breech end than at the muzzle, so they rarely exploded. They could fire both shells, which were useful in attacking wooden ships, and deadly 170-pound (77-kg) balls that could penetrate the hulls of ironclads. The *Monitor,* which took on the Confederate *Merrimack* in the first battle of the ironclad ships, was armed with two Dahlgren cannon.

On the Mississippi River, naval forces used mortars mounted on small flat boats, called mortar schooners. These 8-inch (20-cm) mortars with barrels only about 22 inches (56 cm) long were used during the Siege of Vicksburg to send shells high over the cliffs into the beleaguered town.

Chapter Five

Wartime Innovation

The Civil War could be said to mark the beginning of modern weapons. It was a period of change from old, traditional ways of doing things to new technologies still in use today.

TORPEDO AHEAD!

An important weapon in the Confederate fight was the floating mine. They called it a torpedo, a name that has since come to mean an underwater missile. The idea of torpedoes, or floating mines, was developed by Confederate general Gabriel Rains, George Rains's brother. He was ultimately placed in charge of a Torpedo Bureau, with responsibility for blowing up Union ships to keep them from entering large southern rivers.

Rains's initial mines consisted of small gunpowder-filled barrels floated into the river at the end of long

A drawing of a specific floating mine, or "submarine infernal machine," found in the Potomac River

electrical wires fastened to the bank. Some barrels rode just below the surface, attached to anchors. Others were glass bottles partially filled with powder and floated in the water. At the end of the war, Rains claimed to have sunk fifty-seven ships with his torpedoes—more than were sunk by other, more ordinary weapons.

Because the South mined most rivers, the Union developed a special net that could be cast ahead to haul in any floating mines. They also attempted to make very heavy rafts that could be attached to the bow of a ship and strike the mines. When they tried this technique, though, the exploding raft itself damaged the ship.

Ships called rams were equipped with a pointed iron-clad end with which the sailors could ram another ship, hopefully sinking it. Some rams had spars out front that held torpedoes. When a torpedo-equipped ram crashed into the hull of an enemy craft, the torpedo was supposed to explode, inflicting additional damage.

LITTLE DAVID AT WAR

The Confederates built the first torpedo boat, called the CSS *David,* at Charleston. The *David* was a 50-foot (15.2-m) steam-driven craft, pointed at both ends, and loaded with ballast (heavy material) to make her ride low in the water and be hard to detect. Attached to one end was a spar carrying a 100-pound (45.4-kg) torpedo.

On October 5, 1863, it succeeded in seriously damaging the *New Ironsides.* Twice more the special craft attacked blockading ships, but it had no more successes.

THE AMAZING BUT FAULTY SUBMARINE

In the North, the battle between the *Monitor* and the *Merrimack* prompted the development of a vehicle that

A Confederate torpedo boat was designed to ride low in the water so that it could sneak up on a Union ship.

could be propelled underwater by rowing men. Divers from the submarine could climb out underwater and attach explosives to the vulnerable bottom of a ship covered in iron.

The Union's first attempt, the USS *Alligator*, never made it into battle. It sank in a gale on its way to Charleston. The Confederacy made two attempts with never-tested vehicles called *Pioneer* and *Pioneer II*. They featured snorkel-like devices that brought fresh air into the craft.

THE SINKING OF THE ALBEMARLE

The Union's major success with a torpedo boat came on October 28, 1864. The CSS *Albemarle,* an ironclad designed for work in the shallow North Carolina sounds, had been ramming Union gunboats since the previous spring. William B. Cushing, known for his considerable daring, put together a volunteer crew to sail a small boat right under the ram-clad bow of the troublesome *Albemarle,* which was being repaired at Plymouth, North Carolina.

Under continuous fire, Cushing succeeded in getting his torpedo, mounted on a 14-foot (4.3-m) spar, right under the ironclad. He pulled one line that released the torpedo to nestle up against the ship's hull, then another one that set off the bomb. The explosion of the torpedo sank the *Albemarle* in the shallow water, where it remained until after the war.

The USS Housatonic *sinking after attack by the* H. L. Hunley

Horace Hunley of Mobile, Alabama, built a submarine out of an old boiler for the Confederates. But the *H. L. Hunley* sank the first four times it was tested. In 1864, off Charleston, its spar-mounted torpedo worked magnificently, sinking the USS *Housatonic,* a blockader.

Who won? The *Housatonic* sank in shallow water, allowing most of its crew to climb onto the rigging and be rescued. But the *Hunley* and its crew sank, bringing the total lives lost in the experiment to thirty-six, including that of Horace Hunley. The strange little craft went down in the record books as being the first submarine to sink a ship.

RAPID FIRE

The biggest problem with longarms, or shoulder weapons, was the slowness of reloading. Many inventors worked on the idea of a rapid-fire gun.

Throughout the war, the Confederates used a small weapon called the Williams Rapid-Fire Gun, developed by R. S. Williams of Kentucky. As a hand crank was turned, a cartridge was fed from a hopper into the breech and the percussion cap was struck. It fired about twenty rounds a minute.

The Williams Rapid-Fire Gun

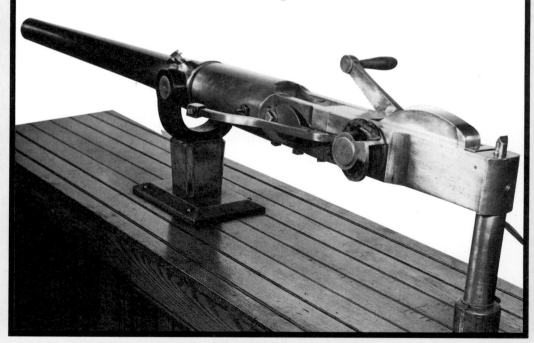

*The Billinghurst-Requa Battery, with twenty-five barrels
that fired separately*

The Union's "coffee-mill gun," the Billinghurst-Requa Battery, had a hopper at the top, filled with shells. These fed one by one into a drum from which they fell into twenty-five separate rifled barrels, which fired in sequence. Abraham Lincoln liked what he saw in a demonstration of this gun and ordered several, but his Chief of Ordnance was reluctant to order such a new-fangled weapon.

Continuous attempts to develop a machine gun eventually led to the more successful Gatling gun. Patented by Richard J. Gatling in 1862, the gun had six barrels that fired in rotation around a central axis. It was not accepted for military use until just as the war was ending.

MINES AND TIME BOMBS

General Gabriel Rains's floating mines also changed land warfare. A few land mines had been used in the Crimean War fifteen years earlier, but Rains turned them into a regular weapon consisting of artillery shells buried below ground. When stepped on, a percussion cap was set off, exploding the device and seriously injuring anyone in the vicinity.

Another type of mine designed by the Confederate Secret Service was a bomb, or grenade, shaped like a chunk of coal. A saboteur could sneak it onto a coal barge, where it would be shoveled into the coal bunker of a ship. At some time during the process—preferably once the ship was at sea—the device would explode.

Land mine development led to the design of the "time bomb." One such bomb, set to go off with the movement of a clock, was sneaked onto an ammunition ship at City Point, Virginia, where it exploded, killing many people.

Apparently, both Confederate and Union top ranks regarded these devices as "ungentlemanly" and opposed their use. The Confederates decided it was all right to use mines in roads where they might stop a pursuit, but it was wrong to use them just to kill the enemy.

INVENTION BECOMES COMMONPLACE

As the Civil War started, American military men used weapons and ideas based on old European models. But as it ended, nations around the world were looking to the United States for new ideas.

Today's submarines, aerial reconnaissance vehicles, and long-distance weapons may seem to bear little resemblance to the primitive devices of the Civil War. Each generation has, of course, made its own refinements. But modern warfare still uses weaponry that originated in the creativity of soldiers, North and South, seeking to win the United States' only civil war.

MAJOR EVENTS OF THE CIVIL WAR

1860
December 20   South Carolina is the first southern state to secede from the Union.

1861
February 4   Representatives from the seceding states meet in Montgomery, Alabama, and form the Confederate States of America.

February 18   Jefferson Davis, previously U.S. Secretary of War, is inaugurated as president of the Confederate States.

April 12   War begins at 4:30 A.M. by a Confederate attack on Union-held Fort Sumter in South Carolina.

April 15   President Abraham Lincoln calls for 75,000 volunteers to help stop the war with the Confederacy.

April 19   Lincoln orders a naval blockade of southern seaports.

July 21   The First Battle of Bull Run (or Manassas) in Virginia is the first important battle; it is won by Confederate troops.

August 10   The Battle of Wilson's Creek in Missouri, another Confederate victory, brings lands west of the Mississippi into the war.

1862
February 16   The fall of Fort Donelson in Tennessee to General Ulysses S. Grant's Union troops opens up Nashville to capture; Nashville becomes the first southern city to be taken by the North.

March 9   The first battle of ironclad ships, the *Monitor* and the *Merrimack* (called the *Virginia* by the Confederacy), ends in a draw but revolutionizes naval war warfare.

April 25   New Orleans, Louisiana, is captured by a fleet under the command of David Farragut.

September 4   General Robert E. Lee's Confederate troops move into Maryland, invading the North for the first time and heading toward Pennsylvania.

September 17   Lee's advance is stopped by the Battle of Antietam (or Sharpsburg) in Maryland, in the war's bloodiest day of fighting.

1863
January 1   The Emancipation Proclamation is signed, granting freedom to all slaves within the seceded states.

March 3   The U.S. Congress approves the conscription, or draft, of all able-bodied males between the ages of 20 and 45.

May   The first all–African-American regiment in the Union army, the 54th Massachusetts, begins serving.

June 3   Lee begins another advance into the North.

June 9   The Battle of Brandy Station in Virginia turns into the largest cavalry action of the War; the North is forced to retreat.

58

July 1–3	The Battle of Gettysburg in Pennsylvania ends Lee's attempt to take the North. From this time on, the Confederates fight a defensive battle within their own states.
July 4	The siege of Vicksburg, Mississippi, ends in a Union victory.
July 8	Port Hudson, Louisiana, surrenders, effectively cutting the Confederacy in half as the Union takes control of the entire Mississippi River.
July 13–16	Riots in New York City protesting the draft kill or injure hundreds.
November 19	President Lincoln delivers the Gettysburg Address as a dedication of the national cemetery at Gettysburg, Pennsylvania.

1864

March 10	General Grant is put in charge of the entire U.S. Army.
August 5	The Battle of Mobile Bay in Alabama is won by the Union fleet under Admiral Farragut.
September 1	The Union army, under General William T. Sherman, captures Atlanta, Georgia.
October 19	After more than two months of fighting in the Shenandoah Valley of Virginia, General Philip Sheridan's cavalry regiments take the valley in the Battle of Cedar Creek, leaving the Confederates without an important source of food or a place to regroup.
November	General Sherman's army marches the 300 miles (483 km) from Atlanta to the Atlantic Ocean, living off the land and destroying everything the Confederates might find useful.

1865

March 13	Out of desperation, the Confederate Congress votes to recruit African-American soldiers. Five days later, the Confederate Congress no longer exists.
April 2	Richmond, Virginia, the capital of the Confederacy, falls to the Union.
April 9	Lee surrenders to Grant at Appomatox Court House in Virginia.
April 14	Abraham Lincoln is shot by southern sympathizer John Wilkes Booth. He dies the next day.
December 18	The Thirteenth Amendment to the Constitution, abolishing slavery, goes into effect.

FOR MORE INFORMATION

FOR FURTHER READING

Hakim, Joy. *War, Terrible War.* A History of US, Book Six. New York:
    Oxford University Press, 1994.

Durwood, Thomas A., et al. *The History of the Civil War.* 10 vols. New
    York: Silver Burdett, 1990.

Tracey, Patrick. *Military Leaders of the Civil War.* American Profiles series.
    New York: Facts on File, 1993.

VIDEOS

The Civil War. 9 vols. Produced by Ken Burns. PBS Home Video.
The Civil War. 2 vols. Pied Piper.

CD-ROMS

African-American History—Slavery to Civil Rights. Queue.
American Heritage Civil War CD. Simon & Schuster Interactive.
Civil War: Two Views CD. Clearvue.
Civil War—America's Epic Struggle. 2 CD set. Multi-Educator.

INTERNET SITES

Due to the changeable nature of the Internet, sites appear and disappear very quickly. The resources listed below offered useful information on the Civil War at the time of publication. Internet addresses must be entered with capital and lowercase letters exactly as they appear.

The Yahoo directory of the World Wide Web is an excellent place to find
    Internet sites on any topic. The directory is located at:
    http://www.yahoo.com

The Internet has hundreds of sites with information about the Civil War. The United States Civil War Center at Louisiana State University maintains a Web site for the gathering and sharing of information:
http://www.cwc.lsu.edu

The Civil War in Miniature by R. L. Curry is a collection of documented facts and interesting tidbits that brings many of the different facets of the Civil War together:
http://serve.aeneas.net/ais/civwamin/

The National Park Service maintains sites on hundreds of Civil War battles. The directory of these sites is at:
http://www.cv.nps.gov/abpp/battles/camp.html

One site specifically on the Battle of Mobile Bay is at:
http://www.mnf.mobile.al.us/area_history/battle.html

The Hunley Web Site contains information on the CSS *H. L. Hunley* submarine, such as where and when it sank, how the bodies were recovered, and how the torpedo worked:
http://members.aol.com/litespdcom/index.html

INDEX

About the Author

Jean F. Blashfield is a writer with more than fifty books to her credit. Most of them are for young people, covering many subjects from chemistry to women inventors to England to World War II. She also has written several fantasy adventure stories and retold the stories of Gilbert and Sullivan operettas. She developed the American Civil War series for Franklin Watts with her husband, Wallace B. Black.

A graduate of the University of Michigan, Ms. Blashfield has been a book editor for many years. She developed three encyclopedias for young people, wrote educational materials about space for NASA, and created the Awesome Almanacs of various states for her own publishing company.